M000164780

SEVEN
LASTING
WORDS

SEVEN LASTING WORDS

JESUS SPEAKS FROM THE CROSS

CHRISTOPHER R. SEITZ

ILLUSTRATED BY HELEN FIRTH

Westminster John Knox Press
LOUISVILLE
LONDON • LEIDEN

Book design by Sharon Adams
Cover design by Pam Poll Graphic Design
Cover illustration by Helen Firth

First edition
Published by Westminster John Knox Press
Louisville, Kentucky

This book is printed on acid-free paper that meets the American National Standards Institute Z39-48 standard. ∞

PRINTED IN THE UNITED STATES OF AMERICA

01 02 03 04 05 06 07 08 09 10 — 10 9 8 7 6 5 4 3 2 1

Library of Congress Cataloging-in-Publication Data
Seitz, Christopher R.
    Seven lasting words : Jesus speaks from the cross / Christopher
R. Seitz.—1st ed.
        p. cm.
    ISBN 0-664-22425-3 (alk. paper)
    1. Jesus Christ—Seven last words—Sermons. 2. Lenten
sermons. 3. Anglican Communion—Sermons. 4. Sermons,
English—21st century. I. Title.

BT457 .S45 2001
232.96'35—dc21

                                                            2001026301

CONTENTS

Foreword

The most moving Christian experience of my school years was the Good Friday service at Christ School, an Episcopal boarding school in the mountains of western North Carolina. The liturgy was traditional: three hours long (noon to three), with stations of the cross and short meditations on the last seven words of Jesus. On that one day of the year, at three o'clock, the daily Angelus ringing from the St. Joseph's Chapel tower was replaced by a solemn, lonely peal of the bell, thirty-three times. This, we were told, marked the years of Jesus' life on earth, his mission ended on a cross on a hill far away. After that, all time was marked by his years, not his by ours.

Looking back on it, I am now struck at how much scripture the liturgy contained and set forth. It was not until much later that I learned to disengage the book of Lamentations, much of Jeremiah and the Psalms, and those compelling lines from Isaiah called the "suffering servant song" (about an innocent, righteous servant from the days of the prophet Isaiah) from the Friday we were told was Good and from a man who lived not in the Old Testament (or did he?) but the New.

No amount of embarrassed, restless twitching and uncooperation from fellow teenaged boys could put us off, at least at some point during the three hours, from the reality that a man was going to his death in a courageous, moving, and extraordinarily efficient manner. I believe that the hardest heart in the chapel knew this was not a death like any other death, and for that reason alone, it was somehow tied up with our life and our death and our destiny below those cross timbers we stared up at, bearing their strange human burden. Was this the fruit of a different tree, and was it the fruit of our sin and the fruit of our own fresh start, all at the same time? Most of us would not have known how to answer the question then, but I believe we all knew that day that the question was being posed. It would take time and our own struggles with sin and failure to see the truthfulness of Good Friday in a way neither ironic nor restless nor past, but plain, arresting, and present forever.

When years later, in graduate school in New Haven, I was ordained and making my way through a similar liturgy in a new place, I saw what it must have looked like to the boarding school chaplain all those years ago. I can still awkwardly make my way through the complex singing part that halted, after a rising and falling of "and when the centurion," on Matthew's final "surely this was the Son of God." What remained over the years was the scripture-laden character of the service, though I missed the straightforward preaching of my old boarding school chaplain. The chaplain back then had learned the service when he was himself a student at Christ School, from 1940–45. I can recall his telling me that his father helped him work through the complex liturgy, a bit strange for his low-church blood. "From generation to generation" as the Good Book says. That was certainly true in his case.

So across the sea, in yet a later time and place, when the local parish asked me to preach on Good Friday, I did not try to come up with something fresh. The idea of finding a fresh angle on Good Friday struck me as foolish, if not somehow offensive, given the riches to which I had been exposed in my life in the church. Good Friday is not a day for novelty. So I adopted the traditional "Last Seven Words" format. I want to thank my father for providing sample texts and three-hour service formats for me to compare. The Rev. James Hiles, my doctoral student here in St. Andrews, also supplied materials from his sturdy files.

Many people have helped make this book possible. I want to thank the congregation and townspeople who turned out to hear me preach at St. Andrews Parish, St. Andrews, Fife on Good Friday 2000. I want to thank my Divinity School students here, who force me to straddle academic and preaching vocations. The book likely would not have appeared had not Helen Firth stepped forward and wondered, "What would I think?" about sketching an illustration or two. I acknowledge her work with gratitude and deep appreciation. Carey Newman at Westminster John Knox is a kindly taskmaster with a shrewd eye. And finally, those who read these brief meditations will not have the opportunity to hear what I heard on that Good Friday 2000: the brilliant Alan Torrance filling out our prayers and meditations from his violin. His rendition of "Schindler's List" and allied themes kept us all on plot that day. No wonder God has seen fit to bring an Institute for Theology, Imagination, and the Arts to this wee village, on our fine Faculty of Divinity at St. Andrews University.

This book is dedicated to my Christ School classmates and their chaplain from 1965–1976, Thomas Comstock Seitz.

Christopher R. Seitz
Good Friday, 2001

"Father, forgive them."

✤✤✤ • ✤✤✤

Two others also, who were criminals, were led away to be put to death with him. And when they came to the place which is called The Skull, there they crucified him, and the criminals, one on the right and one on the left. And Jesus said, "Father, forgive them; for they know not what they do."

Luke 23:32–34

✤✤✤ • ✤✤✤

First Word:

"Father, forgive them."

Two others also, who were criminals, were led away to be put to death with him. And when they came to the place which is called The Skull, there they crucified him, and the criminals, one on the right and one on the left. And Jesus said, "Father, forgive them; for they know not what they do."

A lot of people were put to death by crucifixion at the time of Jesus, so much so that the place was referred to by shorthand as "The Skull."

The Old Testament reports that the condemned were stoned outside the city. Stoning both socialized and anonymized capital punishment, thus enforcing a grisly but just punishment. Then the body was buried. Only for heinous crimes was the body impaled on a tree. If left unburied, the birds, the sun, and nature would go to work until only bones and a skull were left. More deaths, more bones, more skulls—until one day economy of expression produced, on a hill outside of Jerusalem that itself resembled a human head, "the place which is called The Skull." Deuteronomy had reckoned impalings a sign of God's curse and so had stipulated that the corpse must be buried on the same day.

So when Jesus climbed the hill that day the specific justice of Deuteronomy got mixed up with other schemes for execution. Only the later Holocaust could find a way, in addition to the usual concern for torture and efficiency, to do lab work on the doomed victims. Deuteronomy regarded a divine curse nothing to trifle with, and the bodies were buried before sundown. But not so, apparently, at the placed called The Skull.

It is significant that the Gospels all record Jesus' death as unique and, at the same time, banal. All three men that day climbed the same hill, in the same way, one struggling for breath at one minute and another at another. But all three had identical lungs and the same bruised feet and shoulders and shared confusion about what horrors awaited them, about when the pain would be great or less great or unbearable. All could have had

4

relatives who accompanied them, though whether this made things worse, or better, is hard to say. No lightening bolt would deflect the hammer that drove home the nails for Jesus; no charioteer would ride up and rescue him. All three men were equally dead by sundown.

For the soldiers or those who made a sick career out of witnessing death (as true then as now) that Friday was just another day.

What made the death exceptional was supplied by Jesus, with words like these first in a litany of seven: "Father, forgive them." The exceptional couldn't have just been read off the person of Jesus, as an unusual or particularly innocent victim. The name of innocent victims, before that day and long after it, is legion, and in no way could it be said of Jesus' death that he was uniquely mistreated or that his dying outdid all other deaths in terms of pain or loneliness or senselessness. When later the criminal contrasts his deserved death with that of Jesus, he is speaking words that ring true through all time and all places and that demonstrate root injustice that has never faded from human history.

Nor is Jesus' nobility of character entirely without

peer. The annals of human recording tell particularly moving stories of courage and selflessness and even profound insight into the mystery of unjust dying and innocent sacrifice.

Corrie Ten Boom, the famous Dutch evangelist, survived the Holocaust, and she spoke of many such noble figures in the death camps. She herself recorded how difficult it was, once free, for her sister to forgive her persecutors. She spoke of how her sister resented Corrie's own capacity to forgive and to receive Christ and his benefits in the sacraments. She would go up to the altar rail with Corey but keep her hands tightly clenched.

Corey reported in her Christian testimony that the worst part of the death camps was forfeiting all privacy, of being paraded around naked and scoffed at and abused. Of having lost all claim to herself. Of how her life became a place of the skull.

When asked how she could go on afterwards, how she could receive the sacrament and forgive her enemies, she said something like this, "I finally realized that in all the depictions of Jesus on the cross, the little strip of cloth across his waist was just an artist's touch. When Jesus was crucified, there was no little strip of cloth. Where I went in the death camps, Jesus had been before me." Here is the New Testament truth, that "God made him to be sin who knew no sin, that in him we might become the righteousness of God." Jesus exposed all secrets that day, all hidden evil, all the worst things we keep to ourselves and hoard and do not give him. On Good Friday, nothing was hidden, all was exposed. "God made him to be sin who knew no sin, so that in him we might become the righteousness of God."

On account of this man, one day Corrie looked over at her sister, there beside her at the altar rail, and saw her hands open and tears streaming down her cheeks.

What makes Jesus different and this day good has nothing to do with us. This is the day when we have nothing to give and everything to receive, when we can weep or unclench our hands and let Jesus speak his word of forgiveness again. This is a day when our place is to open our hearts and let him in where we have shut him out—this past year, this past season, or all our lives, in one way or another. Good Friday means to catch us off guard with its Savior climbing the hill again.

It is Luke who records Jesus praying on our behalf, "Father, forgive them." He does not look down from the cross, find his supporters, and explain how his death fits into God's plan for them, who have right along been loyal and good. Fourth Maccabees, an intertestamental book, records the martyrdom of the aged Eleazer, who prayed before he died, "Thou knowest, God, that though I might have saved myself, I die in fiery torment for the Law. Make my blood an expiation for them, and take my life as a ransom for theirs."

Jesus' death contains a theological explanation, but it is not that. His prayer is not an explanation but an invitation and an embrace. We do things and think things and, even in our best piety and actions, do not, from Jesus' point of view, truly know what we do. We are those who crucify our Lord for the very best of reasons, not just for reasons of obvious evil or fear or hostility toward love undeserved.

But what makes Jesus our Lord is his capacity to see us out of infinite love and patience and then say, as he is climbing a hill and hanging from a cross, "Father, forgive them, for they know not what they do."

Only this power of God can open hands to receive and eyes to see anew, washed by tears of gratefulness and forgiveness.

"Today you will be with me in Paradise."

＊➤➤ · ➤➤＊

One of the criminals who were hanged railed at him, saying, "Are you not the Christ? Save yourself and us!" But the other rebuked him, saying, "Do you not fear God, since you are under the same sentence of condemnation? And we indeed justly; for we are receiving the due reward of our deeds; but this man has done nothing wrong." And he said, "Jesus, remember me when you come into your kingdom." And he said to him, "Truly, I say to you, today you will be with me in Paradise."

Luke 23:39–43

＊➤➤ · ➤➤＊

Second Word:

"Today you will be with me in Paradise."

O ne of the criminals who were hanged railed at him, saying, "Are you not the Christ? Save yourself and us!" But the other rebuked him, saying, "Do you not fear God, since you are under the same sentence of condemnation? And we indeed justly; for we are receiving the due reward of our deeds, but this man has done nothing wrong." And he said, "Jesus, remember me when you come in your kingly power." And he said to him, "Truly, I say to you, today you will be with me in Paradise."

The most forceful religious statements are often no more than self-protection or acts of simple desperation. The first criminal boldly confesses that Jesus is the Christ, when any number have failed to see this in Luke's Gospel and are doubtless unconvinced now as Jesus hangs on the cross.

There is, of course, this *religious* part of us that Satan

can spot in the best of us, as was the case with Job. Part of us is prepared to serve God because it has to its favor expectation of reward. Take away the blessing, and the good and righteous Job will curse you, Satan says. There is no such thing as disinterested piety—as loving God for God's own sake. "Are you not the Christ? Save yourself—*and us*!"

The Greeks knew this well, too. Gods were in the business of making transactions. If one proved weak or ineffective, the religious observer knew it was time to take his business elsewhere. In that sense, religion was utterly practical. I need things. I beseech this god to help and move to another if I need to.

The criminal makes a proposal alongside his confession. In so doing he reveals the religious mind at work: "I'll take a semi-risk, pay Jesus an honorific, but if I do, I want something for it." And the mocking odor of his confession is defense in case his risk proves vain.

This religious instinct, born of human nature and different from faith given from above, Calvary exposes. Calvary exposes all the lies we cherish, those that keep us from dying and rising with this man Jesus. The Goodness of Good Friday includes the wisdom of the former

14

U.S. president, Harry Truman, who once remarked, "I don't giv'em hell. I tell them the truth and it sounds like hell." Calvary tells the truth about innate human religious instincts: that they are self-serving and cannot soar with the joy and cleansing power God means to bestow in the cross of Christ.

Here at Calvary, the lie of the criminal, the lie of our religious self, is not exposed directly by Jesus. It is the other criminal who speaks up and gives us a gracious and loving mirror in which, God willing, we might view ourselves. "Jesus, remember me."

Luke does not portray a vindictive or vindicating Jesus but rather a silent, strong, and gracious Jesus. Jesus does not speak out against his accusers, even as he warns of a darkness yet to come. Neither does he respond to the thief. In the silence, then, space is created for a response from you and me. A response, not of innocence, nor of objection, nor of justification, but of simple acknowledgment that we have nowhere to stand apart from this man and his destiny, whatever it may finally be. "Jesus, remember me."

So the criminal speaks to Jesus for us. Before this

man Jesus, the truth of ourselves is laid bare, and the thief sees this, that we deserve due reward for our deeds, in the logic of our human systems. Yet in this man Jesus we see nothing deserving death or punishment. So it must be that some transfer—is it divine or is it demonic?—is taking place. Something is moving from us to him, and someone is moving it. In this space, we, like the criminals, must make a choice. And even then, it is not clear whether we are choosing Jesus or whether we are given to see that he has chosen us: "that the Lord laid upon him the iniquity of us all."

Where does this right speech come from? This speech from the criminal, when he says, with such simple need, "Jesus, remember me." What gives him the strength to turn now back to himself and see some hope, in the face of such mockery and sadness, in this Jesus enduring a cruel punishment no different from his own? I think it would be far simpler now to say, "Let's go down together. Sometimes bad things happen to good people. At least someone carried your cross."

Instead the thief is given eyes to see. To see that in Jesus things are different, are being made different. To see that from here on out there is a hope against hope. To see that today is not like any other day but can only be described as the day we are to be with him, this suffering and yet triumphant Jesus, forever, in Paradise. With him who stooped and in so doing conquered.

"Truly I say to you, today you will be with me in Paradise."

When we hear words like these we must realize—we can even hope the bargaining religious criminal with his counterpart in us realizes—that we are confronting the "One with whom we have to do" (Heb. 4:13). And with that realization our bargaining, religious tongue is set free to say, maybe against our better judgment, "Jesus, remember me."

For that is all it takes, all it has ever taken—given the offering of this man—to turn a tide that has been running out for as long as we can remember, a tide that swaps over and runs back in the instant we hear his strong promise: "Truly I say to you, today you will be with me in Paradise."

"Woman, behold your son."

❧❧❧ · ❧❧❧

Standing by the cross of Jesus were his mother, and his mother's sister, Mary the wife of Clopas, and Mary Mag'dalene. When Jesus saw his mother, and the disciple whom he loved standing near, he said to his mother, "Woman, behold, your son!" Then he said to the disciple, "Behold, your mother!" And from that hour the disciple took her to his own home.

John 19:25b–27

❧❧❧ · ❧❧❧

Third Word:

"Woman, behold your son."

S tanding by the cross of Jesus were his mother, and his mother's sister, Mary the wife of Clopas, and Mary Magdalene. When Jesus saw his mother, and the disciple whom he loved standing near, he said to his mother, "Woman, behold your son!" Then he said to the disciple, "Behold your mother!"

Well, it was not an easy time, I am sure. We have intruded on a very private moment—this personal exchange between the man raised high up and the family at his feet.

The Gospels never dwell on the precise physical agonies or the mechanics of death on a cross. Cicero said that crucifixion was the most ghastly form of torture ever invented. We have had to leave it to archaeologists and movie makers to supply the details: whether the nails went through hands or forearms, feet or ankle bones. What percentage never survived the beatings, administered in the usual dark cell, somewhere in the sewer line of human engineering, meant to wear down the victim. Whether the little seat designed to support the naked body and prolong the torture was dispensed with in Jesus' case. The Gospels show in even fashion a Jesus climbing the hill of death. They do not omit the pain but in many cases describe it only to show how the psalms and sacred scriptures of Israel, with their words of preparation, were here, in Jesus, finding their final resting place. They were fulfilled, that is, filled to their fullest expression at last, by an intention calibrated before the foundations of the earth, before the calling of Abraham, the giving of the Law, the sending of the prophets.

It has been said that the strongest proof of the virgin birth lies in the heart of Mary, who with a word could have named Jesus' father and so destroyed his claim to be God's son. In the language of accusation as John's Gospel records it, "We have a law, and by that law he ought to die, because he has made himself the Son of God." And so the sword must pierce her heart as well this day, who knew from the beginning what secrets this man's life would disclose.

He had said, had he not, that he would come and

would divide families—fathers from sons and so also it follows, a son from his mother. But what of Mary? What of the disciple whom he loved, who is not family at all? They are parting his garments and giving them away, leaving Jesus with nothing. Are they parting his family too, rending it into torn and tattered pieces, with this awful death? Must the psalms be fulfilled here too, when they say, "My friends and companions stand aloof from my plague, and my kinsmen stand afar off"—and is Jesus actually seeing to their fulfillment with these words of his from the cross?

Poor Mary. What she has endured. What the birth of this son has cost her, and how her heart could still break somewhere in some recess, after she was sure it could not break any more.

I'm not sure we are meant to try to soften this. Are there not times in the life of faith when the billows and waves of sheer heart-brokenness overwhelm and flood out all sense? I suspect this was such a moment for the disciple whom Jesus loved and for his mother. By his very act of giving the one to the other, he was saying goodbye forever as the one they had known as friend and son, and yet who was never these things in any simple sense. That anguish too belongs to the sacrifice of the cross of Christ: a testimony to the fragile character of those things we hold most dear when all is lost. "At least I have my family," the victim of earthly grief proclaims after the tornado has leveled everything. "At least I've got my family"—this too belongs to the offering of Jesus, for us, and indeed for Mary and the disciple whom he loved who may for a moment be dazed with grief.

In the novel *The Last Temptation*, Nikos Kazantzakis makes a noble effort to see the loss of family and friends as that which was most torturous to Jesus—the "temptation too far." So he lets Jesus come down from the cross and live out his life. In a moment of insight, however, Kazantzakis sees that such an act on Jesus' part would have set loose, in its wake, enormous suffering and hopelessness. Kith and kin, important though they are, can never accomplish what Jesus is accomplishing in this act of love. Seeing this, and experiencing its awful reality, the aged Jesus makes his way back to Calvary and gives himself over to the act of love and holiness it was his destiny to fulfill. The "last temptation" is foiled.

"WOMAN, BEHOLD YOUR SON."

No one sees this better than John in this precious scene of leave-taking. John, who is himself likely the beloved disciple, took Mary to his own home as of that very hour.

It is not clear that the greatest temptation we must face is holding our families in higher regard than Jesus. Many of us find families a hardship and a trial, as indeed they are. There would be no point in sentimentalizing Jesus, his mother, and his beloved friend, and the Gospels never play on this such that the sacrifice of Jesus becomes intensely personalized or a matter of his overcoming human affections or desires.

This is why the act of separation from kith and kin is genuinely the creation of a new family. Mary and John are genuinely mother and son, brother and sister, beloved friend and ones whom Jesus loved and who now love one another as he loves us. The beloved disciple, we are told, takes Mary home. Whatever tears they shed that night, they shed under the shadow of a new day, a new hope, and a complete reconstituting of what family means in Jesus Christ.

*"My God, my God,
why hast thou forsaken me?"*

＊＊＊ · ＊＊＊

*And about the ninth hour Jesus cried
with a loud voice, "Eli, Eli, la'ma sabach-
tha'ni?" that is, "My God, my God, why
hast thou forsaken me?"*

Matthew 27:46

＊＊＊ · ＊＊＊

Fourth Word:

"My God, my God, why hast thou forsaken me?"

And about the ninth hour Jesus cried with a loud voice, "Eloi, Eloi, la'ma sabach-tha'ni?" that is, "My God, my God, why hast thou forsaken me?"

Jesus's cry of dereliction is the most piercing cry of the Bible. It must be heard with utter seriousness. It is loud and it is real, the most real thing that ever was.

From the sixth hour to the ninth hour, the noon-to-three of this day's service, darkness fell over the land. Three full hours of waiting, listening, with the volume knob of his receiver turned all the way up, to God's silence and absence. Three hours of mounting physical anguish, and now absolute moral and spiritual darkness. In the words of Karl Barth, Jesus now "goes into the far country." He goes to that place we would all go, must all go, forfeit of God's holy love, watching the scales tip in the direction of sin and sorrow. We would have at last no way to load the other pan, and watch the scales right themselves and with relief see them fall on the side of our righteousness and goodness and merit.

"My God, my God, why hast thou forsaken me?" is what it means for Jesus to hear the pan hit bottom on the wrong side, to crash down from a height and with a weight he had imagined but now must experience more than anything he has known before. There is no statement to rival this one from Jesus in all the Gospels. This one is spoken, not to us, but for us. Not to his friends, but for them. Not to anyone but to his own silent Father in heaven. A dark and silent heaven for an hour long eternity.

Jesus goes into the far country and what he encounters there he encounters for us. He goes straight into a void we have made in the way of Adam. He goes into the darkness that is a creation mishandled, left to rot and decay, from our selfish disregard. He goes into the darkness of God's silence, because God cannot live where his holiness and goodness are mocked, cannot for his own sake. "Holiness is the eternal moral power of God," P. T. Forsyth wrote, "which must do, and do, till at last it sees itself everywhere." "You shall be holy, as I am holy" is the word of a God who so cares for us and all he has made that he demands we be like him, so we can be with him as he is, today and forever and ever. Only a God who does not care allows his creatures to sin and gives no thought to the consequences. As though consequences did not count, were not real. When the puppy knocks over the milk dish we forgive the puppy, but someone must clean up the spilled milk. It is the way of God's good universe. Only a God who cares provides, out of love, his own self, in his own son, and asks him to walk into the far country of our making, and so let his light shine there—a light we cannot make or recover from a lost Victorian innocence—until all is bright and new.

> O generous love! That he, who smote
> In Man for man the foe,
> The double agony in Man,
> For man should undergo.

The double agony of perfect love, holy love, and utter

dereliction, utter abandonment, is here working in one Man for man.

In a novel by John Irving, Owen Meany is dogged by an intuition. He must be prepared in three ways he does not understand, ways that are to the world strange, and he cannot set aside this odd compulsion placed within his breast. He is a small, misshapened boy, "with no beauty that we should desire him," as Isaiah might have put it.

Through his growing years and through a stint in Vietnam and into middle age, he still practices the same strange drills, not knowing what they mean: one involving the use of his voice, which is otherwise brittle and lacking in respect; one involving the hurtling of others high in the air toward a basketball goal; and one involving his strange size and skill with language.

Then one day, in midlife, he is at the airport, and there is a terrorist attack. A racist gunman is loose, and Owen finds himself trapped in a bathroom with a group of young kids visiting from Asia. The three skills "prepared for him to walk in" suddenly find their logic and their appointed home. He takes charge, his small size and practiced voice perfect for the task. His army language skills kick in. He organizes the frightened boys in a long queue and one by one tosses them up through a high window, in rapid fashion, to a nun who is their leader on this outing gone wrong. The last one pops through to safety as the gunman bursts through the door. Owen at last knows who he is, and what all the preparation was about, before his final moment.

The words that Jesus speaks in the far country were used words, not new ones. They had rattled through the centuries, through the years of Israel's walk with God. Jesus knew these words. He may have wondered if one day he would say them, and not be reciting a psalm in worship, with another to follow, and another after that, and then out to a fresh new day. If one day he would be speaking the language of all Israel, all creatures, for all time. For in this one moment that would end all cries of dereliction, he lifted us to freedom on the back of his loss and abandonment into God's silence and judgment, making it impossible to hear Psalm 22 or Isaiah 53 again as language from someone's past but instead as language prepared for Jesus to walk in, to walk into the far country, for us. Now when we go there, as indeed we must, he is there waiting for us with his eternal arms of love and cleansing, healing wounds. For us. Making Psalm 22, in double agony, Jesus' majestic song of love unknown. A love unknown until now, and now shining from him from every pore.

"I thirst."

After this Jesus, knowing that all was now finished, said (to fulfil the scripture), "I thirst." A bowl full of vinegar stood there; so they put a sponge full of the vinegar on hyssop and held it to his mouth.

John 19:28–29

Fifth Word:

"I thirst."

After this Jesus, knowing that all was now finished, said (to fulfil the scripture), "I thirst." A bowl full of vinegar stood there; so they put a sponge full of the vinegar on hyssop and held it to his mouth.

Matthew, Mark, and John all record that, before he died, Jesus was offered vinegar to drink by those who were there watching.

In Matthew and Mark, several bystanders took the cry of Jesus, "Eloi, Eloi," to be a cry for Eli-jahu (Elijah, the prophet). One of these bystanders ran quickly and fetched a sponge and filled it with vinegar, and offered it to him to drink.

The connection of these two things in Matthew and Mark—the vinegar and the expectation of Elijah—may mean that the drink was intended to buy Jesus more time before he died so he could continue to call for Elijah.

Many felt that Elijah's return signaled the end of all things, the final chapter, the return of the Lord God Jehovah himself, as promised in the prophet Malachi.

On other occasions the vinegar was given to half-unconscious victims so as to prolong the torture. Cruel smelling salts. Here, to the contrary perhaps, it would turn the crucifixion of Jesus into something meaningful beyond itself. The crucifixion of Jesus would prove different, not because of what God was doing in him, but because his death would be the occasion for a more important religious event: the dramatic return of the prophet Elijah, as promised in the last verses of the Old Testament.

Jesus, however, refuses the drink. He was not calling on Elijah. He was calling on God, the God he identifies with his foresakenness. The cry of dereliction was not to be misunderstood as pointing to some other religious truth. It was what it was for the purpose God intended for this man.

The significance of the vinegar is seen differently by John, though in a way very much related. Jesus' use of Psalm 22 was meant to signal that his death, and the precise terms of it, even down to details, was in accordance with God's will from eternity. Even at the point of his cry of abandonment, Jesus was abandoned into language prepared for the occasion. His absolutely unique experience of God's judgment and absence was described with language already at play in Israel's experience of God. Jesus used borrowed words for a completely unborrowed moment, borrowed from no time ever before and from no time ever since.

John communicates the same sense of destiny in far less dramatic fashion: not with language borrowed from the unmistakeable first line of Psalm 22, nor with the highly detailed imagery of Isaiah 53. With the simple expression of need, "I thirst," Jesus understands his impending death as taking place "in accordance with the scriptures." With reference to the most basic human need, Jesus senses his hour has come and that he has arrived at a moment prepared from eternity. As in Matthew and Mark, Jesus knows the vinegar has nothing to do with Elijah. It has nothing to do with dulling his senses. It has nothing to do with what those who offer it think they are doing. It has nothing to do with making his death into something sensible beyond itself.

Jesus sees into this moment of dereliction. He sees abandonment and silence, the double agony. But he also hears, inside the agony, confirmation, again from the Psalms that were his hymnal and his scriptures, a line now numbered verses 20–21 of Psalm 69:

> I looked for pity, but there was none;
>> and for comforters, but I found none.
> They gave me poison for food,
>> and for my thirst, they gave me vinegar to drink.

But now, the language of the Psalms is robbed of any potential tragedy. Because Jesus speaks these words and sees them as confirmation of God's hand upon him, in wrath and in holiness, they also mean that something is being finished forever. Tied up. The anguish of Jesus fits. It fits into Jesus' final conviction, a conviction that alone makes this day good beyond measure, a conviction that not just we believed but *he believed* it was for us, he hung and suffered there. What we must come to see, from within the broken wreck, the dogged hopefulness, the hope/despair, hope/despair, tick/tock pendulum swing of our natural life, Jesus sees for himself that day at the final moment. And knowing that all was finishing up, he spoke forth words we have all said before. That we said as soon as we could talk and that may well be among the last words we speak: "I'm thirsty." But on this occasion those words are spoken that the scripture might be fulfilled, spoken that we might know Jesus knew what he was doing, because he knew what God was doing in him, in his anguish, in his loneliness, and in his final basic cry for something to ease his thirst. When that sponge came up, and he smelled the vinegar, he saw in the moment something no other psalmist had seen: the final accomplishment of God's plan for salvation, forever and ever and ever.

"It is finished."

When Jesus had received the vinegar, he said, "It is finished"; and he bowed his head and gave up his spirit.

John 19:30

Sixth Word:

"It is finished."

W hen Jesus had received the vinegar, he said, "It is finished"; and he bowed his head and gave up his spirit.

In the movie *The Last Temptation of Christ*, Jesus decides to come down from the cross and live out his life, with a wife and family, into ripe old age. It is a grim scenario, however. So much so that one student who watched the film in a class I teach likened this time of Jesus on earth as a descent into hell. Another called it purgatory. What Jesus was meant to have accomplished he *has not* accomplished, and the world is very much the worse for it. Even Judas realizes that Jesus is a coward—that what was required of the Messiah he has not followed through on.

In a final scene we learn that it was all a dream conjured up by exhaustion and the devil. Jesus finds himself back on the cross, genuinely relieved. We can almost hear him in John's triumphant key: "For this I was born, and for this I have come into the world, to bear witness to the truth." The truth to which Jesus has come to bear witness is his life and death as a sacrifice for our sins. John's portrayal is helpful because in it we never see a Jesus who believes, no matter how anguished he becomes, that there is any other road to follow than the one he is following. So, in a way, it is helpful to see in this final scene of the movie the tortured place the world is and how tortured Jesus is with his final sacrifice missing.

There is an American film, very popular at Christmas time, called *It's A Wonderful Life*, with Jimmy Stewart and Donna Reed. Depressed and at his wits' end from financial ruin and humiliation, Stewart's character seeks to take his life. In a vision he is shown what the world looks like with him absent. He visits in on his family, his town, his church, his friends. And he learns that the world has become a sadder and more desperate place without him and that he is powerless to change things. His absence has not been neutral but has been felt and felt keenly. The world longs for his presence and for his goodness and patience, and he sees how selfish and pointless was his suicide. He awakens a new man and, even in financial ruin, gives thanks for all he has been given and all it has been his lot to give.

It has become commonplace, but important nonetheless, to stress that "it is finished" does not mean, in Greek, "whew, that is over with." It means, "it is accomplished; the ball has found the goal; the point of it all has at last been made, and made good on forever and ever."

"And he bowed his head." It is possible here to see every prior bowing of Jesus' head—in private prayer; in attention to a small, unnoticed detail; in sober consideration of what lay before him; in public prayer before healing, or teaching, or worship—all as foreshadowings of this final bowing of his head. His accomplishment on this day had its same obedient love and purpose on every day of his life.

When Jesus gives up his spirit here, it does not float into a void, as the last breath of life goes forth when we die. Nor is this a spirit that leaves and looks back wistfully on what life could have been, or in sadness at what his early death left undone. Jesus here gives up his spirit that we might receive it and might, in so doing, live the life of accomplishment he has prepared for each of us to walk in.

The purpose of Jesus' accomplishment is not only the removal of our sin and stain by offering himself, for us, to his Father. It is that, but it is more. The accomplishment of Jesus brings something to an end—our death and despair in Adam—and with one stroke it also brings something new, the gift of his life, of his spirit, for us, for our present lives in him.

There is a certain artificiality in separating Good Friday from Easter, if pushed too hard. This dying, it must be said, only brings one thing to a close so that another might be set in motion. There must be a perfect offering, and there is in him. But the perfect offering is offered to clear something away, permanently, finally, surely, perfectly. When the spirit is yielded up, it is yielded to the Father, just like the pleasing sacrifice of Noah. And it is received by him with affection for us, with the promise of a new day, every bit as dramatic as the change from flood to dry and fruitful land, and more so.

We cannot imagine with what angle of vision Jesus looked down on the world God had made and for which he now gave up his spirit. But we can be sure he looked down that last moment aware that this creation was being changed forever by his action. That this creation was being claimed as his own good creation and was being rescued from every stain and every sad blemish afflicting it East of Eden. There would be no way Jesus could speak of accomplishment and mean that we were to build a shrine at Calvary and look back on this death with nostalgia and thanksgiving without also having our entire vision and sense of ourselves and the world dead with him and brought back to new life again. Accomplishment of the sort Jesus effected on Calvary leans as much forward as backward. As much ahead toward our eternal home with him forever and ever, beginning here and now, as behind, in the mopping up of every sin and stain, as far back as the flaming sword guarding the way to the tree of life. For that tree has become this cross, and that sword has been sheathed, and we are free now to lean into his death and find there our life. What is finished is a life whose only purpose was and is to give us new life and new hope, a living hope, and peace with our Father in Heaven. When Jesus says, "It is accomplished," he has this in mind and nothing less.

"Father, into thy hands I commit my spirit."

❧❧❧ · ❧❧❧

It was now about the sixth hour, and there was darkness over the whole land until the ninth hour, while the sun's light failed; and the curtain of the temple was torn in two. Then Jesus, crying with a loud voice, said, "Father, into thy hands I commit my spirit!" And having said this he breathed his last. Now when the centurion saw what had taken place, he praised God, and said, "Certainly this man was innocent!" And all the multitudes who assembled to see the sight, when they saw what had taken place, returned home beating their breasts. And all his acquaintances and the women who had followed him from Galilee stood at a distance and saw these things.

Luke 23:44–49

❧❧❧ · ❧❧❧

Seventh Word:

"Father, into thy hands I commit my spirit."

And the curtain of the temple was torn in two. Then Jesus, crying with a loud voice, said, "Father, into thy hands I commit my spirit." And having said this he breathed his last.

Luke continues this account of Jesus' death with an immediate confession from the centurian standing there, who praised God and declared Jesus innocent. For Luke, the centurian is a representative figure. He is the point and goal of Jesus' death; he is the one like us Jesus seeks to lay claim to, and does, immediately, here in this scene. There is an unbroken movement from Jesus' death to its claim to be a death for us, and it belongs to the mystery of Good Friday that its most essential truth is ratified by Easter and not disclosed over against it.

Indeed, John suggests that had the disciples understood the scriptures, they would have seen that every clock that was ever set at any place in the universe was here at the moment of death being reset to the time of God's eternity.

This is why it is completely right to call Good Friday "Good" and not intend by that some lurking irony.

The most important thing about the crucifixion is that it destroys whatever gap we might have suspected existed between God and his complete disclosure of himself to us. It destroys the idea that God would be truly God if we could just get at him more fully—get behind his words, behind the scriptures, behind the testimony to him, behind whatever it is that we believe is both disclosing and hiding him at the same time.

The sin of Adam was the belief, rising up as an overpowering suggestion from the created realm itself, that there was a God behind the God who had spoken to him. It was the belief that there was a God about whom it could be said, "That is the real God and that is what he really said and what he is really like."

In a moment of inspiration, Bonhoeffer characterized the question "Did God say?" and had the serpent pose it in the garden this way:

The misleading thing about this question is that it obviously wants to be thought to come from God. For the sake of the true God it seems to want to sweep aside the given Word of God. Beyond this given Word of God the serpent pretends somehow to know something about the profundity of the true God who is so badly misrepresented in this human word. The serpent claims to know more about God than man, who depends on God's word alone. The serpent knows of a greater, nobler God who does not need such a prohibition. In some way (the serpent) wants to be itself the dark root from which the visible tree of God then springs up.

Hanging on the tree of Calvary is God as he really is, and there is defeated forever the claim that he can be known behind something that reveals and obscures him at the same time. Defeated is the devil's claim to know who the real God is, behind his word to us. Calvary allows the devil and human sin to play its most potent card, and in so doing to show that God has put forth himself, in his son, as the means by which he can be fully known, loved, trusted, and obeyed—obeyed with an obedience granted East of Eden, by the Spirit released in Jesus' last breath.

There is no gap. And because there is no gap the devil can no longer suggest there is some other way to find the true God who gives life by dispensing fruit from some tree we have yet to see. This is the tree of life, this cross of Jesus. This is the place where knowledge of good and evil and eternal life are no longer opposed. They have been taken up and reconciled by the new Adam. For the final answer to Pilate's question, and the question posed in every disguise the devil has ever adopted—What is truth?—we must now look no further nor be beguiled into searching anywhere else than right here.

Isak Dinesen writes imaginatively of the return of Christ for his eternal reign:

> At the time when the near return of Christ to earth had become a certainty, a Committee was formed to decide upon the arrangements for His reception. After some discussion, it sent out a circular which prohibited all waving and throwing about of palm branches as well as all cries of "Hosanna."

> When the Millennium had been going on for some time, and joy was universal, Christ one evening said to

Peter that He wanted, when everything was quiet, to go out for a short walk with him alone.

"Where do you want to go, my Lord?" Peter asked.

"I should like," answered the Lord, "just to take a walk from the Praetorium, along that long road, up to the Hill of Calvary."

We can assume that, even for Jesus, this was his finest hour—the moment of which he was most proud. And now, with the generosity it is his to display, he who has defeated all pretense and sham on that holy tree shares the moment with the one who was frightened and denied him.

That is also a sharing with you and me, and that is the tree of life on the hill of our peace and reconciliation.

The Temple curtain is torn down the middle, and there can be no doubt anymore about where God is to be seen and worshiped and loved. It is here; it is for us. And it is for him his finest hour, our eternal joy and peace.

"I should like just to take a walk from the Praetorium, along that long road, up to the Hill of Calvary."

And as he goes, he takes our hand. And we feel there the wounds, and we sense they are somehow familiar. But there has been a balm in Gilead, and the healing that pours from those wounds is so great we catch our breath and stumble for a wee moment. But he lifts us up and we go on and when we arrive and look back down we see before us the Garden of Eden, and God's voice is sure and we are sure it is his, as the Holy Spirit tends to some flowers, with wolf and lamb lying down beside him.

Behold, the wood of the cross, how it has made all things bright and clean. "It turneth all to gold, for that which God doth touch and own cannot for less be sold."

AMEN